OTHER GIFTBOOKS IN THIS SERIES

baby boy
hope! dream!
love
A Mother means home
birthday!

Published in 2015 by Helen Exley® in Great Britain.

Edited by Helen Exley
Illustrations © Joanna Kidney 2015
All the words by Pam Brown, Helen Exley and Stuart & Linda Macfarlane
are © Helen Exley Creative Ltd 2015
Design, selection and arrangement
© Helen Exley Creative Ltd 2015
The moral right of the author has been asserted.

ISBN 978-1-84634-946-1
12 11 10 9 8 7 6 5 4 3 2 1

Printed in China

Helen Exley Giftbooks,
16 Chalk Hill, Watford, Herts, WD19 4BG, UK.
www.helenexleygiftbooks.com

Follow us on and

Irish Blessings

PICTURES BY JOANNA KIDNEY

Helen Exley®

May good luck be your friend
In whatever you do.
And may trouble be always
A stranger to you.

A little health,
a little wealth,
a little house and freedom.
And at the end,
a little friend,
and little cause to need him.

AUTHOR UNKNOWN

CELTIC BLESSINGS

May the strength of the wind and the light of the sun,

The softness of the rain and the mystery of the moon

Reach you and fill you.

May beauty delight you and happiness uplift you,

May your step be steady and your arm be strong,

May your heart be peaceful and your word be true.

May you seek to learn, may you learn to live,

May you live to love, and may you love – always.

Here's a health to thine and thee,

not forgetting mine and me.

When thine and thee again meet

mine and me,

may mine and me have as much welcome

for thine and thee

as thine and thee

have had for mine and me tonight.

IRISH TOAST

May the light shine out
of the eyes of you,
like a candle set in the
window of a house,
bidding the wanderer to come in
out of the storm.

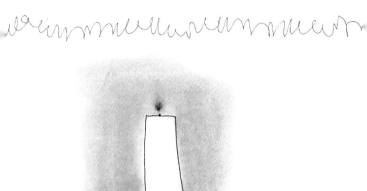

Walls for the wind

and a roof for the sun,

And drinks by the fire.

Laughter to cheer you

And those you love near you

And all that your heart may desire!

And though these

sheltering walls are thin,

May they be strong to keep hate out,

And hold love in.

LOUIS UNTERMEYER 1885 – 1977

For each petal on the wild flower
  Each brings a wish your way.
Good health, good luck
    and happiness
  For today and every day.

May you find little paths bright with sunshine, hedged with flowers.

PAM BROWN 1928 – 2014

Good luck to us al

nd bad luck to nobody.

Bless you and yours
    As well as the cottage you live in.
May the roof overhead
            be well thatched
    And those inside
                well matched.

May the road rise to meet you.
May the wind
be always at your back.
May the sun shine warm
upon your face,
The rains fall soft
upon your fields.
Until we meet again.

May your children
and your children's children laugh.
May the years bring peace
to every one of you.

HELEN EXLEY

Deep peace, pure white of the moon to you;

Deep peace, pure green of the grass to you;

Deep peace, pure brown of the earth to you;

Deep peace of the running wave to you,

Deep peace of the flowing air to you,

Deep peace of the quiet earth to you.

FIONA MACLEOD 1855 – 1905

A BLESSING

May the lilt of Irish laughter
lighten every load.
May the mist of Irish magic
shorten every road.
May you taste the sweetest
pleasure that fortuned e'er bestowed,
And may all your friends
remember all the favours
you are owed.

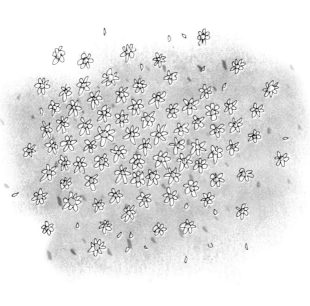

A BLESSING

May the day never burden.

May dawn find you awake and alert,

approaching your new day with dreams,

possibilities and promises.

May evening find you gracious and fulfilled.

May you go into the night blessed,

sheltered and protected.

May your soul calm, console and renew you.

JOHN O'DONOHUE 1956 – 2008

May every road
be easy
on your feet.

PAM BROWN 1928 – 2014

AN IRISH PRAYER

For every storm, a rainbow,

For every tear, a smile,

For every care, a promise,

And a blessing in each trial.

For every problem life sends,

A faithful friend to share,

For every sigh, a sweet song,

And an answer for each prayer.

May your life
be blessed
with long springs
and short winters.

HELEN EXLEY

May joy and peace
surround you,
contentment latch your door,
And happiness
be with you now,
and bless you evermore.

May the longtime sun
shine upon you,
all love surround you,
and the sweet light
within you
guide you on your way.

HEALTH OF
THE NIGHT'S SLEEP
TO YOU!

THE MOONBEAM TOAST

I wish you quiet sleep, good

dreams, happy awakenings.

PAM BROWN 1928 – 2014

May the luck of the Irish
possess you.
May the devil fly off
with your worries.

Between us and the little people,

Us and the people of the wind,

Us and the evil hour of temptation,

Us and the drowning power of water,

Us and the earth's withering breath,

Us and the slave's cruel death...

May the roof above you
never fall in
And may us good companions
beneath it
Never fall out.

May the raindrops fall

lightly on your brow.

May the soft winds

freshen your spirit.

May sunshine

brighten your heart.

May the burdens of the day

rest lightly upon you.

I wish you days
of sunshine –
and only enough rain
to sweeten the fruit
and plump the grain.

PAM BROWN 1928-2014

How small the boat
in which each life sets sail;
how great the oceans
and the dangers.
May the sunlight touch the wave tops
that shift and shimmer.
May clean wind take your sails.

MAY THE HAND OF A FRIEND

ALWAYS BE NEAR TO YOU.

Bless this house, O Lord we pray
Make it safe by night and day.
Bless these walls, so firm and stout,
Keeping want and trouble out.
Bless the roof and chimney tall
Let thy peace lie over all
Bless the doors, that they may prove
Ever open to joy and love...

HELEN TAYLOR, FROM "BLESS THIS HOUSE"

A following wind,
a gentle sea,
a bright and constant star,
And at the end,
safe haven.

PAM BROWN 1928-2014

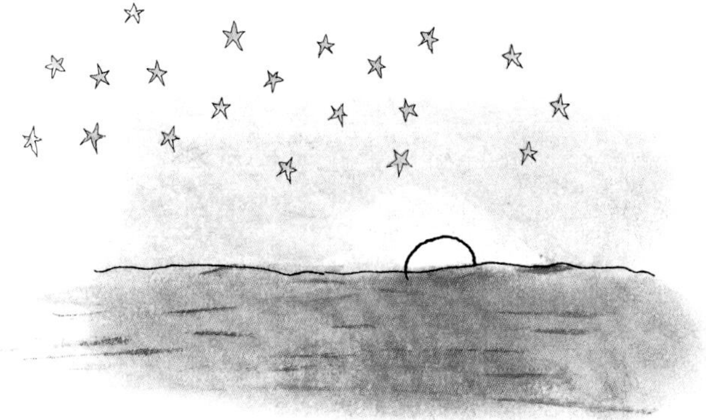

MAY YOU EVER TRAVEL

NEW PATHWAYS,

EXPLORE DISTANT HORIZONS

AND AT THE END

OF LIFE'S JOURNEY

COME SAFELY BACK HOME.

IRISH TOAST

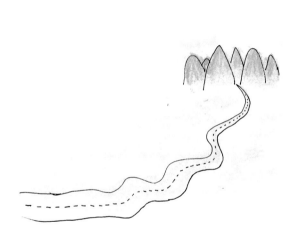

May you have lots of friends.
May those friends
       give you love and care
and kindness
       for all your days.

HELEN EXLEY

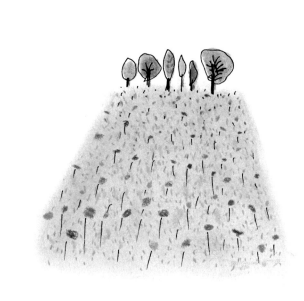

May the frost never
afflict your spuds.
May the outside leaves of your cabbage
always be free from worms.
May the crows never
pick your haystack,
If you inherit a donkey,
may she always be in foal.

IRISH TOAST

May you have a full moon
on a dark night
and the road downhill
to your door.

May the light of friendship guide
Your paths together.
May the laughter of children grace the halls
Of your home. May the joy of living
for one another trip a smile from your lips.
And when eternity beckons, at the end
Of a life heaped high with love,
may the good Lord embrace you
With the arms that have nurtured you
the whole length of your joy-filled days.

May the blessing of light be on you,
light without and light within.
May the blessed sunshine
shine on you and warm your heart
till it glows like a great peat fire,
so that friend and stranger may come
and warm themselves at it.

May your days be filled

with rainbow days.

STUART & LINDA MACFARLANE

Bless my humble kitchen;
I love its every nook.
Bless me as I toil in it
About my daily work.
Bless the meals that I prepare
Grant seas'ning from above.
Bestow Thy blessing and Thy grace
And most of all, Thy love.
Let us not forget
all those who enter here;
Bless them
with joy and peace and love.

MAY YOUR HEART BE AS WARM

AS YOUR HEARTHSTONE.

AND WHEN YOU COME TO DIE

MAY THE WAIL OF THE POOR

BE THE ONLY SORROW

YOU'LL LEAVE BEHIND.

MAY GOD BLESS YOU ALWAYS.

MAY THE GOOD LORD

TAKE A LIKING TO YOU.

...BUT NOT TOO SOON!

May you have food and raiment,
a soft pillow for your head.
May you be forty years in heaven
before the devil
knows you're dead!

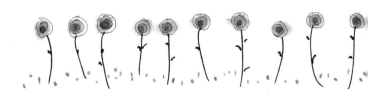

May love and laughter
light your days,
and warm your heart and home.
May good and faithful friends be yours,
Wherever you may roam.
May peace and plenty
bless your world,
With joy that long endures.
May all life's passing seasons
bring the best to you and yours.

IRISH BLESSING

To your good health,
old friend,
may you live
for a thousand years,
and I be there
to count them.

ROBERT SMITH SURTEES 1803 – 1864

When the first light of the sun shines –
Bless you.
When the long day is done –
Bless you.
In your smiles and your tears –
Bless you.
Through each day of your years –
Bless you.

May your thoughts
be glad
as the shamrocks,
May your heart
be as light as a song,
May each day bring you bright,
happy hours,
That stay with you
all the year long.

Helen Exley runs her own publishing company which sells giftbooks in more than seventy countries. She had always wanted to do a little book on smiles, and had been collecting the quotations for many years, but always felt that the available illustrations just weren't quite right. Helen fell in love with Joanna Kidney's happy, bright pictures and knew immediately they had the feel she was looking for. She asked Joanna to work on *smile*, and then to go on to contribute the art for four more books: *friend, happy day!, love* and *hope! dream!* We have now published nine more books in this series, which are selling in 27 languages.

Joanna Kidney lives in County Wicklow in Eire. She juggles her time between working on various collections of illustrations and working as a visual artist. Her card ranges *Joanna's Pearlies* won the prestigious Henries 'oscar' for 'best fun or graphic range'.

Helen Exley Gifts
16 Chalk Hill, Watford, WD19 4BG, UK
www.helenexleygiftbooks.com